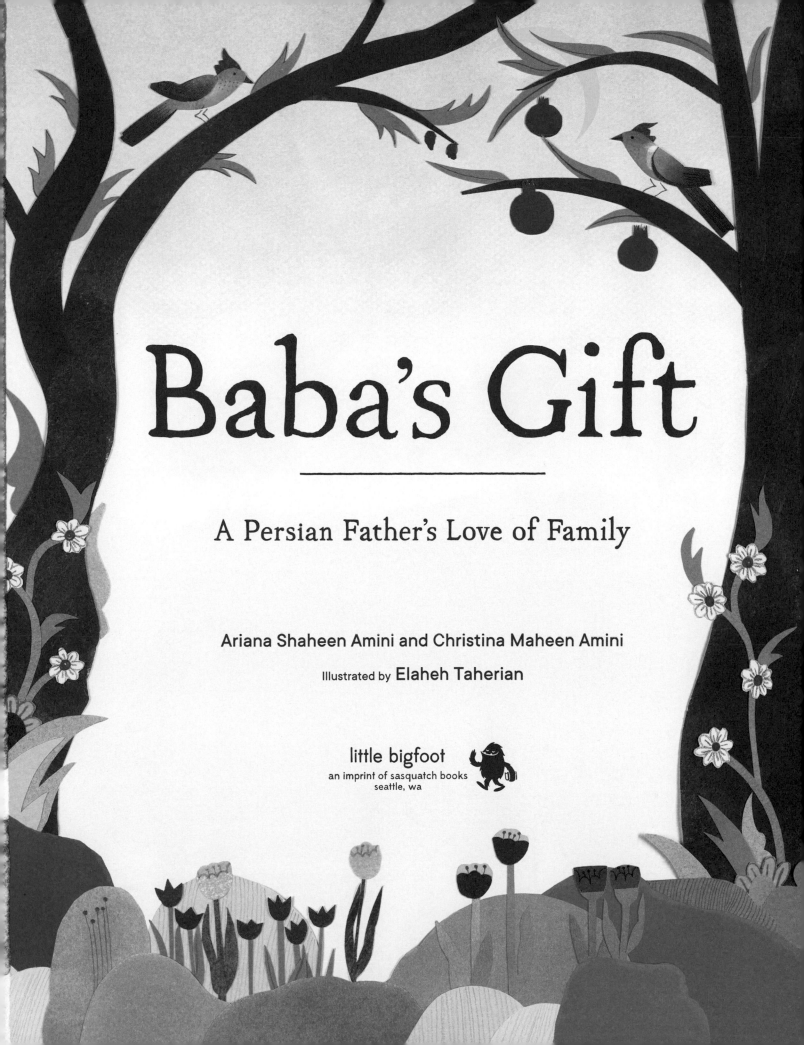

Baba's Gift

A Persian Father's Love of Family

Ariana Shaheen Amini and Christina Maheen Amini

Illustrated by **Elaheh Taherian**

little bigfoot

an imprint of sasquatch books
seattle, wa

I call my dad Baba. *Baba* means "dad" in Farsi.

Baba gave my five sisters and me middle names from his homeland: Shereen for "sweetness," Roshan for "light," Parvaneh for "butterfly," Shaheen for "princess," and Farine after Baba—whose name is Fariborz. I am Maheen. Maheen for "moon."

My sisters and I look up at the moon from our home in California.

Baba says, "This same moon illuminated my nights when I was a boy in Iran."

Baba dances with us on the intricate patterns and flowering vines of our Persian carpet. He lifts us each up and twirls us until we are dizzy. Then he sets us down, and we feel like we are floating.

"Baba, what did your home in Iran look like?" I ask.

He traces the swirling indigo and pomegranate colors of the carpet with his fingers and says, "My childhood home had gardens that looked like this."

My sisters and I imagine ourselves in fragrant gardens of jasmine and roses, skipping between mulberry trees.

Baba says, "The gardens connected my family's houses. Every neighbor was an aunt or an uncle, a niece or a nephew, a cousin or a second cousin."

On warm summer nights, Baba says his family would enjoy dinner outside, eating dishes like saffron rice and *joojeh* kebabs, drinking tea with sugar cubes, and telling stories.

Baba says, "After dinner, we would watch the sunset beyond fields of golden wheat. Then the whole family would take long walks under the moonlit sky."

My sisters and I stand on the carpet, holding hands, and Baba joins us, as if we are walking with his family in Iran.

"Baba, why did you leave your home?" I ask.

He says that as much as he loved his family and his country, he was curious about the rest of the world.

"Every weekend," he says, "I went with my cousins to the cinema. In the American films, all the people were smiling and dancing. I wanted to go there."

He says he wanted to live in the land of possibility. He wanted the best education.

Baba says, "The United States was on the other side of the world, but I begged my mother to let me go."

"Why did your mom let you go?" we ask.

"Because her greatest joy was to make me happy. She knew I loved learning and new challenges." Baba pauses, then says, "And we both thought one day I would return to my home in Iran."

بار
Baggage

When the day came for him to leave Iran, he wore his best suit and looked like a movie star. His mother rolled up a Persian carpet and packed it in his big suitcase.

Baba's family walked him to the airport where he hugged each of them goodbye.

His mother held him in a long embrace. She did not know when she would see him again.

"It was my first time on an airplane," Baba says. "I flew over mountains and tiny cities into the night sky, then soared over the bright-blue Atlantic Ocean."

My sisters and I pretend to fly over our carpet, imagining it is the same large ocean that separates our families.

"When I arrived, no one was waiting to greet me.
I had no family and no friends. I spoke very little
English," Baba says. "All I had was the carpet my
mother had given me."

Baba tells us he soon discovered American life was
not like in the movies. "I was an outsider," he says.

"I wanted to be proud of who I was *and* to be part of
this country."

↗ Gates B 1

← Gates B 17

Gates A 1-16 →

Gates A 17-34 →

✈ Departures →
✈ Arrivals ←
🧳 Baggage ↙

↗ Gates B 1-16

Gates A 1-16 →

← i Information

Farsi - English
English - Farsi
Dictionary

To connect with people, Baba says he worked very hard to learn English.

Baba's voice is rich and deep. His English is beautiful.

His Farsi is beautiful, too. But all I know in Farsi is:

Yek. Do. Seh.
One. Two. Three.

"Why didn't you teach us Farsi?" I ask.

Baba responds, "It was too painful. The language reminded me of all I left behind."

Baba walks to his desk and makes a drawing.

He shows it to us and says, "Each circle in this picture is like a world of its own. I was living in two worlds at once: Iran and Farsi; the United States and English."

He points to the space where the circles overlap and says, "Both worlds share a love of family."

I imagine my dad carrying the love of family in his suitcase, along with his Persian carpet, and unrolling it as a gift to share with each one of us.

"Baba, did you miss your family in Iran?"

"Very much," Baba says. "But I dreamed of becoming a doctor, so I applied to one of the best medical schools in the country." His face lights up. "I was the only student accepted who was not from the United States."

As he studied, new words filled his mind.

Baba says his mother, halfway around the world, beamed with pride for him, and decided to go to law school so that she would be more educated, too.

When Baba talks about his mother, his eyes fill with tears.

My sisters and I gather around our father and say,
"Baba, we wish we could have known your mom."

He gazes at a portrait of his mother, and says, "You know her through my love for you. You know how I say, 'When a child is delighted in, she finds herself delightful.'

"She delighted in me. I delight in you. I was her world. You are mine."

Baba dances with us on the carpet.

"My greatest wish is that when you grow up, you will
live close to each other and your children will play
in the garden. And as you dance together on the
flowering vines of the Persian carpet, you will feel
my love for all of you," Baba says.

My sisters and I listen to Baba.

We dream that we are holding hands, taking moonlit walks from his childhood garden to ours, weaving our worlds together.

For Baba and our family—ASA & CMA

For the memory of my parents
Mihan and Baba—AT

Manufactured in China by C&C Offset Printing Co. Ltd. Shenzhen,
Guangdong Province, in August 2022

LITTLE BIGFOOT with colophon is a registered trademark of
Penguin Random House LLC

27 26 25 24 22   9 8 7 6 5 4 3 2 1

Editors: Michelle McCann, Christy Cox
Production editor: Peggy Gannon
Designer: Anna Goldstein
Photographs: Ariana Shaheen Amini and Christina Maheen Amini

Library of Congress Cataloging-in-Publication Data
Names: Amini, Ariana Shaheen, author. | Amini, Christina Maheen, author. |
  Taherian, Elaheh, illustrator.
Title: Baba's gift : a Persian father's love of family / Ariana Shaheen
  Amini and Christina Maheen Amini ; illustrated by Elaheh Taherian.
Description: Seattle, WA : Little Bigfoot, an imprint of Sasquatch Books,
  [2023] | Audience: Ages: 4–8 | Audience: Grades: K–1
Identifiers: LCCN 2022023555 | ISBN 9781632173232 (hardcover)
Subjects: LCSH: Amini, Fari–Junevile literature. | Immigrants–United
  States–Biography–Juvenile literature. | Iranians–United States–
  Biography–Juvenile literature. | Fathers and daughters–
  United States–Juvenile literature.
Classification: LCC E184.I5 A53 2023 | DDC 305.891/55073092
  [B]–dc23/eng/20220606
LC record available at https://lccn.loc.gov/2022023555

ISBN: 978-1-63217-323-2

Sasquatch Books
1325 Fourth Avenue, Suite 1025
Seattle, WA 98101

SasquatchBooks.com

Authors' Notes

OUR BABA, FARIBORZ AMINI

Fariborz Amini, age nineteen

Fariborz Amini, age seventy

Baba's Gift is the true story of Dr. Fariborz Amini, who was born and raised in Iran. He left his family at age nineteen to go to the United States to attend the University of California, Berkeley. He continued on to medical school at the University of California, San Francisco, where he taught for thirty-seven years. As a doctor who helped adults and children understand their emotions and relationships, Dr. Amini cowrote the bestselling book *A General Theory of Love*. He was an amazing mentor and guide to his patients, students, and colleagues, and spent his life dedicated to authenticity—being true to one's self—and to the importance of the relationships between parents and children.

Baba's family was the world to him. He was their world, too, with his ability to listen deeply and love wholeheartedly. His gift was his extraordinary love for his six daughters, his twelve grandchildren, and his wife. After Baba died, his family had a memorial bench engraved with one of his favorite sayings: "When a child is delighted in, she finds herself delightful."

WRITING *BABA'S GIFT*

When I was pregnant with my first child, I started weekly interviews with our dad, Baba. Sitting in his den with a tape recorder and tea, I loved listening to him tell me about memories of his childhood in Iran. Exactly six months after my son was born, our dad passed away, and I felt an urgency to remember his love and life. This story, *Baba's Gift*, evolved into a collaboration with my sister, Christina Maheen Amini.

—Ariana Shaheen Amini

My older sister Ariana taught me to read at an early age, and from that day on, I have loved the magic of books. *Baba's Gift* began with Ariana's words, and then we collaborated, across coasts and time zones, to celebrate our father, who enchanted us with his stories, transporting us to the land of his childhood in Iran. By sharing this story, we honor our dad, his life, his love, and our family.

We discovered the vibrant work of Elaheh Taherian through WomenWhoDraw.com. We love that Elaheh, like our father, grew up in Iran and immigrated to the United States. She now lives near her sister, just like I do.

—Christina Maheen Amini

ACKNOWLEDGMENTS

Thank you to Alison McGhee, Amy Novesky, Michelle McCann, and Christy Cox for believing in our dad's story.

(From left to right) Christina Maheen, Elita Farine, Ariana Shaheen, Fariborz, Kim Shereen, Dawn Parvaneh, Lisa Roshan

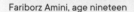